BULLDOZERS

by Aubrey Zalewski

Cody Koala
An Imprint of Pop!
popbooksonline.com

abdobooks.com
Published by Pop!, a division of ABDO, PO Box 398166, Minneapolis, Minnesota 55439. Copyright © 2020 by POP, LLC. International copyrights reserved in all countries. No part of this book may be reproduced in any form without written permission from the publisher. Pop!™ is a trademark and logo of POP, LLC.

Printed in the United States of America, North Mankato, Minnesota

052019
092019

♲ THIS BOOK CONTAINS RECYCLED MATERIALS

Cover Photo: iStockphoto
Interior Photos: iStockphoto, 1, 5, 7 (top), 7 (bottom left), 7 (bottom right), 11, 12, 13, 15, 19, 21; Shutterstock Images, 9, 17

Editor: Meg Gaertner
Series Designer: Jake Slavik

Library of Congress Control Number: 2018964591
Publisher's Cataloging-in-Publication Data
Names: Zalewski, Aubrey, author.
Title: Bulldozers / by Aubrey Zalewski.
Description: Minneapolis, Minnesota : Pop!, 2020 | Series: Construction vehicles | Includes online resources and index.
Identifiers: ISBN 9781532163289 (lib. bdg.) | ISBN 9781644940013 (pbk.) | ISBN 9781532164729 (ebook)
Subjects: LCSH: Bulldozers--Juvenile literature. | Earthmoving machinery--Juvenile literature. | Excavating machinery--Juvenile literature. | Construction equipment--Juvenile literature.
Classification: DDC 624.152--dc23

Hello! My name is

Cody Koala

Pop open this book and you'll find QR codes like this one, loaded with information, so you can learn even more!

Scan this code* and others like it while you read, or visit the website below to make this book pop.

popbooksonline.com/bulldozers

*Scanning QR codes requires a web-enabled smart device with a QR code reader app and a camera.

Table of Contents

Chapter 1

The Bulldozer Can Help!

Construction workers want to build a house. But the ground is too bumpy. A bulldozer makes the ground **level**. Now the workers can start building.

Watch a video here!

Chapter 2

A Bulldozer's Job

Bulldozers do many different jobs. They move rocks out of the way. They spread dirt so the ground is flat.

> Bulldozers **plow** snow in the winter.

Learn more here!

Many people use bulldozers. Construction workers use them to build roads. **Loggers** use bulldozers to remove tree stumps. Farmers use bulldozers to clear fields.

Chapter 3

Parts of a Bulldozer

Bulldozers have a large **blade** in front. Different blades do different jobs. A blade can be used to push, scoop, or dig.

Complete an activity here!

Some blades are straight.

They push dirt out of the way

to make the ground **level**.

Other blades are curved.
They act like shovels. They
scoop up dirt and rocks.

Some bulldozers have a **ripper**. It is like a large claw. The ripper breaks up hard ground. It makes the ground easier to work with.

A bulldozer can have many rippers.

Most bulldozers move
on **tracks**. Tracks keep heavy
bulldozers from sinking into
the mud.

A bulldozer that has
tracks is called a crawler.

blade

ripper

tracks

Chapter 4

Types of Bulldozers

Bulldozers can be big or small. One type of bulldozer weighs as much as 25 elephants! This bulldozer is used for **mining**.

Learn more here!

Some bulldozers move
on wheels instead of **tracks**.
These bulldozers cannot
push very heavy objects.
But they can turn more easily
than bulldozers with tracks.

Making Connections

Text-to-Self

Have you ever seen a bulldozer at work? What was it doing? Where was it?

Text-to-Text

Have you read about another construction vehicle? How is it similar to a bulldozer? How is it different?

Text-to-World

Bulldozers make hard work easier. What are some other tools that make jobs easier?

Glossary

blade – a piece of metal that has a sharp edge.

level – flat.

logger – a person who cuts down trees.

mining – the process of digging rocks or minerals from the ground.

plow – to clear snow from a road.

ripper – a large claw-like tool used to break up hard ground.

track – a metal belt on the bottom of a bulldozer that helps the bulldozer move.

Index